BIG SHIP SMALL SHIP
© 2020 by Galeron Consulting Group.

All rights reserved. Printed in the United States of America. No part of this book may be used or reproduced in any manner whatsoever without written permission except in the case of brief quotations embodied in critical articles or reviews.

This book is a work of fiction. Names, characters, businesses, organizations, places, events and incidents either are the product of the author's imagination or are used fictitiously. Any resemblance to actual persons, living or dead, events, or locales is entirely coincidental.

10 9 8 7 6 5 4 3 2 1
ISBN: 978-1-63514-860-2

For information visit:
GALERON CONSULTING GROUP
PUBLISHING DIVISION
website: www.gcgpublishing.com

The foreman and ship repairman on the dock thought that he was getting help for free. The little boy named Nicky was just hanging around and was excited to go on board, so he didn't even want to get paid for working on the ship. But with the two of them working together, the ship's problems became worse and worse with all the drilling, the sawing and the hammering. Poor Captain!

This book belongs to:

_____

BIG SHIP

SMALL SHIP

COLORING BOOK

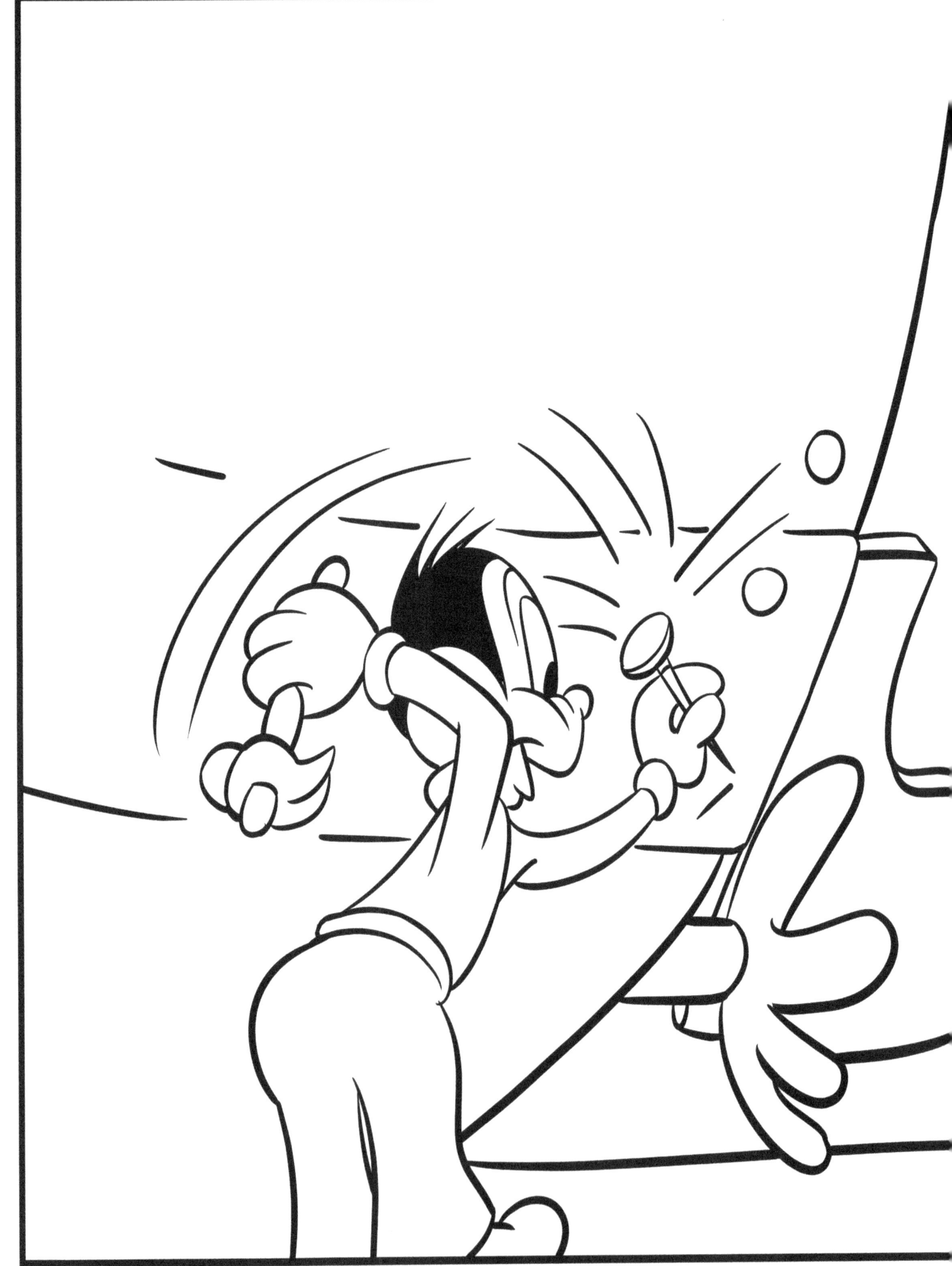